VOCALS

SING 8 FAB FOUR HITS WITH DEMO
AND BACKING TRACKS ONLINE

THE Beatles

PLAYBACK+
Speed • Pitch • Balance • Loop

To access audio visit:
www.halleonard.com/mylibrary

Enter Code
6801-7112-7046-4551

Cover photo courtesy CBS/Photofest

ISBN 978-1-4950-9601-3

7777 W. BLUEMOUND RD. P.O. BOX 13819 MILWAUKEE, WI 53213

In Australia Contact:
Hal Leonard Australia Pty. Ltd.
4 Lentara Court
Cheltenham, Victoria, 3192 Australia
Email: ausadmin@halleonard.com.au

Visit Hal Leonard Online at
www.halleonard.com

COME TOGETHER

Words and Music by JOHN LENNON
and PAUL McCARTNEY

Moderately slow, with a double-time feeling

Here come old flat top, he come groov - ing up slow - ly, he got Joo Joo eye-ball, he one ho - ly roll - er, he got

hair down to his knee. _ Got to be a jok - er, he just do what he please. _

He wear no shoe-shine, he got toe-jam foot-ball, he got mon-key fin-ger, he shoot
He Bag Pro-duc-tion, he got wal-rus gum-boot, he got O - no side-board, he one
He roll-er coast-er, he got ear-ly warn-ing, he got mud-dy wa-ter, he one

Co - ca Co - la, he say, "I know _ you, _ you know me." _
spi - nal crack-er, he got feet down be-low _ his knee. _
Mo - jo fil - ter, he say, "One and one and one _ is three." _

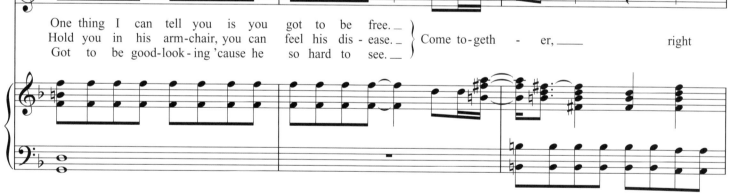

One thing I can tell you is you got to be free. _
Hold you in his arm-chair, you can feel his dis-ease. _ } Come to-geth - er, _ right
Got to be good-look-ing 'cause he so hard to see. _

now, _ o - ver me. _

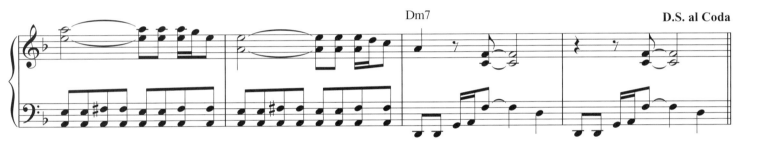

Come to - geth - er, _____ Yeah!

ELEANOR RIGBY

Words and Music by JOHN LENNON
and PAUL McCARTNEY

Moderately fast

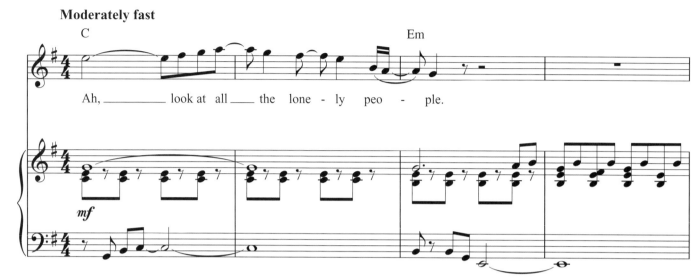

Ah, _____ look at all _____ the lone-ly peo-ple.

Ah, _____ look at all _____ the lone-ly peo-ple.

El-ea-nor Rig - by picks up the rice _ in the church _ where a wed - ding has been, _

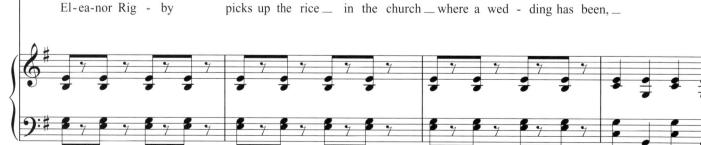

lives in a dream. ___ Waits at the win - dow, wear-ing a face ___ that she keeps ___ in a jar ___ by the door. ___

___ Who is it for? ___ All the lone - ly peo - ple, where do ___

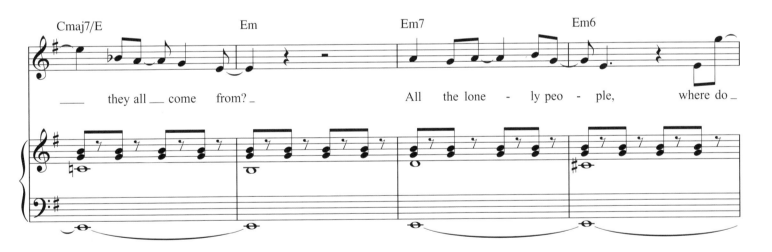

___ they all ___ come from? ___ All the lone - ly peo - ple, where do ___

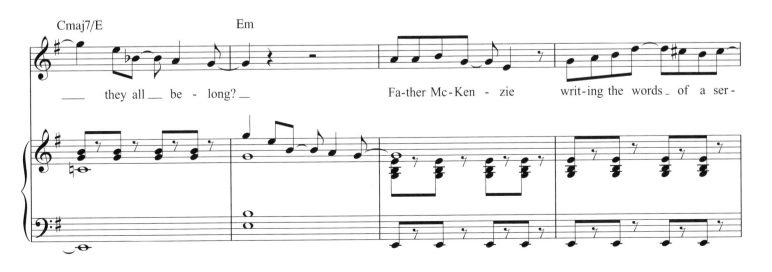

___ they all ___ be - long? ___ Fa-ther Mc-Ken - zie writ-ing the words ___ of a ser -

Ah, _____ look at all ___ the lone - ly peo - ple.

Ah, _____ look at all ___ the lone - ly peo - ple.

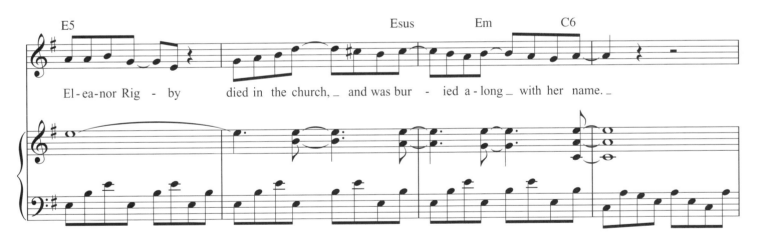

El - ea - nor Rig - by died in the church, _ and was bur - ied a - long _ with her name. _

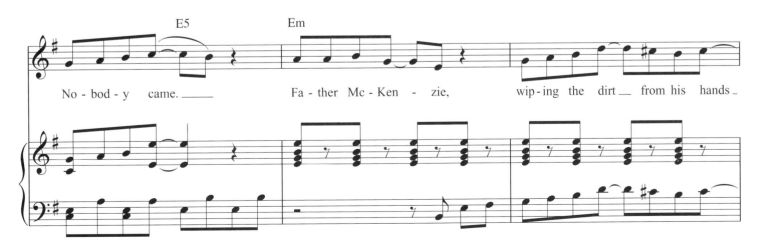

No - bod - y came. _____ Fa - ther Mc - Ken - zie, wip - ing the dirt _ from his hands _

HERE, THERE AND EVERYWHERE

Words and Music by JOHN LENNON
and PAUL McCARTNEY

HERE COMES THE SUN

Words and Music by
GEORGE HARRISON

Here comes _ the sun, ___ dut - n - du - du.   Here comes _ the sun, ___ and I ___ say ___

dut - n - du - du.   Here comes the sun, and I say it's all right.

Sun, sun, sun, here it comes.

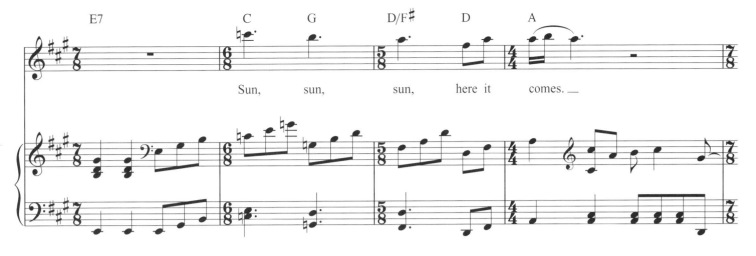

Sun, sun, sun, here it comes. ___

Sun, sun, sun, here it comes. ___

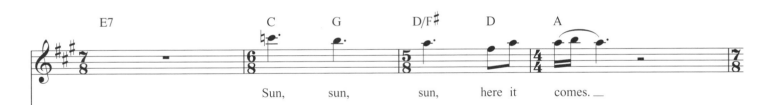

Sun, sun, sun, here it comes. ___

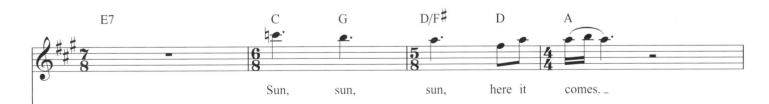

Sun, sun, sun, here it comes. ___

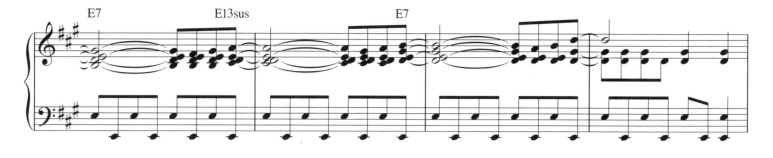

Lit - tle dar - ling, I feel __ that ice __ is __ slow - ly melt - ing.

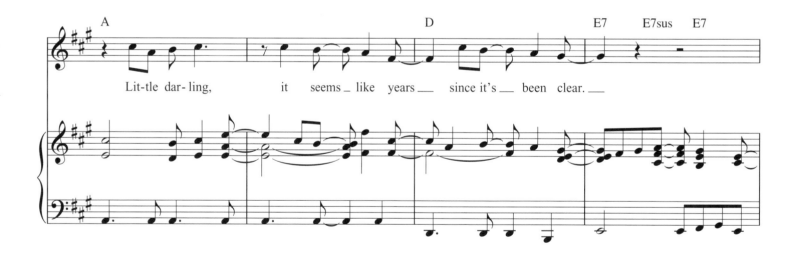

Lit - tle dar - ling, it seems __ like years __ since it's __ been clear. __

Here comes _ the sun, __ dut-n-du-du. Here comes _ the sun, __ and I ___ say

IN MY LIFE

Words and Music by JOHN LENNON
and PAUL McCARTNEY

MICHELLE

Words and Music by JOHN LENNON
and PAUL McCARTNEY

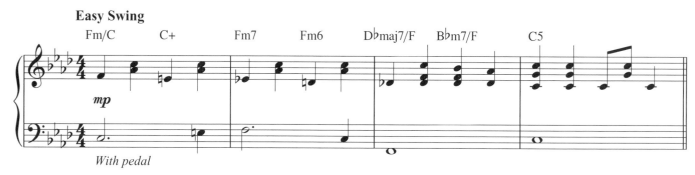

Mi - chelle, _ma belle;_ these are words that go to - geth - er

well, my Mi - chelle. _ Mi - chelle, _ma belle,_

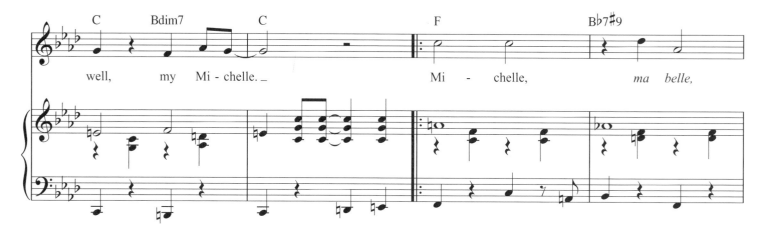

sont les mots qui vont tres bien en - semble, _ _tres bien en - semble._

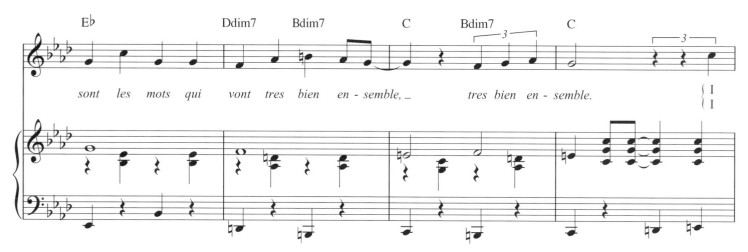

sont les mots qui vont tres bien en - semble, tres bien en - semble. And I will

say the on - ly words __ I know that you'll un - der - stand, my Mi -

chelle. *(Vocal 1st time only)*
Instrumental solo

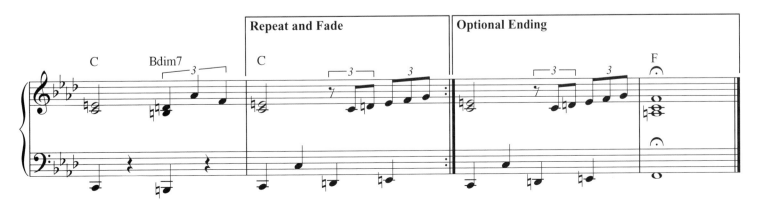

YESTERDAY

Words and Music by JOHN LENNON
and PAUL McCARTNEY

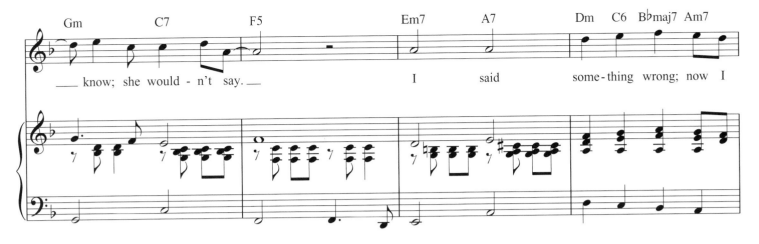

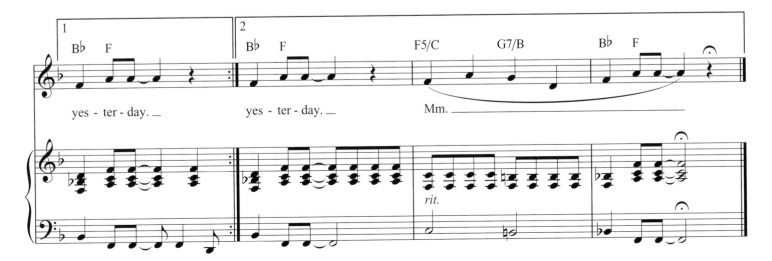

LET IT BE

Words and Music by JOHN LENNON
and PAUL McCARTNEY

Am   Am7/G Fmaj7   F6   C   G

-ing right in front of me,   speak-ing words of wis - dom: "Let it be." __
___   a chance that they will see there will be an an - swer: "Let it be." __
-er Mar - y comes to me,   speak-ing words of wis - dom: "Let it be." __

1
F   C/F F6   C   Am   Cmaj7/G

___   Let it be, _____   let it be,   let it be, _____

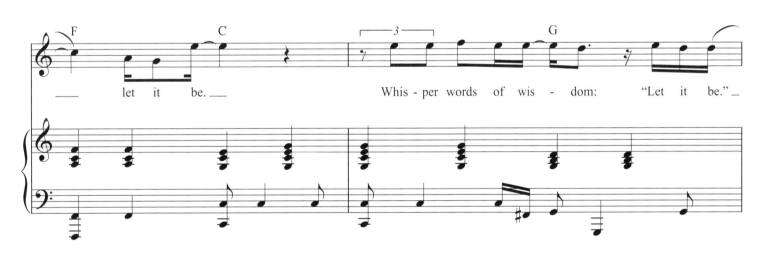

F   C   ⌐ 3 ⌐   G

___ let it be. __   Whis - per words of wis - dom: "Let it be." _

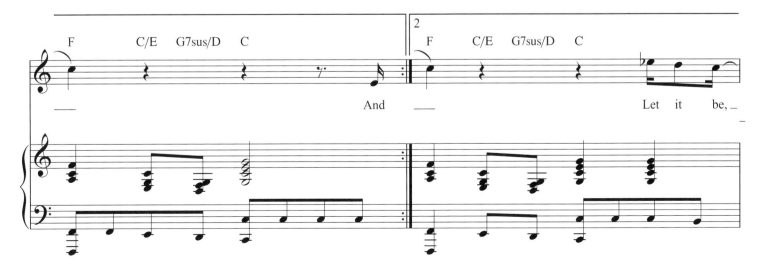

F   C/E G7sus/D C   2 F   C/E G7sus/D C

___   And ___   Let it be, __

Am   Cmaj7/G   F   C

let it be,   let it be, _____   let it be. ___   Yeah,
let it be,   let it be, _____   let it be. ___

G

1
F C/E G7sus/D C

2
F C/E G7sus/D C

there will be an an - swer: "Let it be." ___   Let it be, _ __
Whis - per words of wis - dom: "Let it be." ___

F C/E G7sus/D C B♭ F/A G F C   F C/E G7sus/D C B♭ F/A

Instrumental solo

G F C   C   G   Am   Am7/G Fmaj7 F6

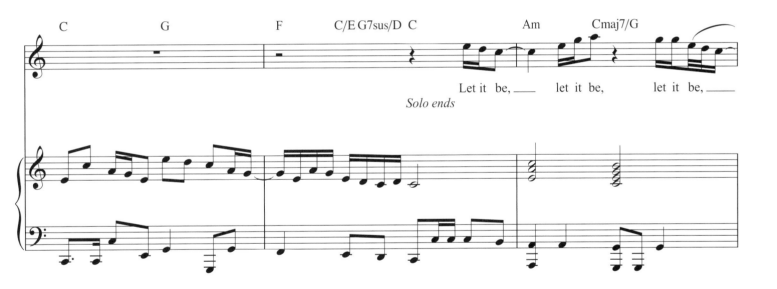

Let it be, ___ let it be, let it be, ___

Solo ends

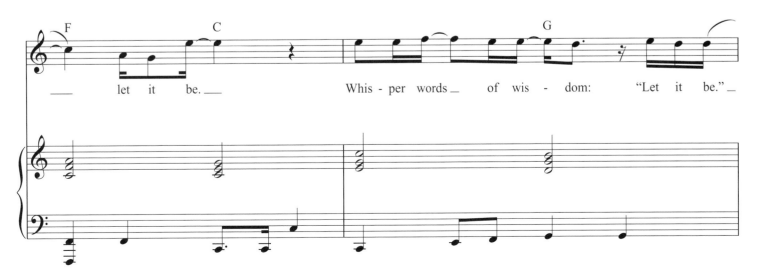

___ let it be. ___ Whis - per words ___ of wis - dom: "Let it be." ___

F   C/E G7sus/D C

D.S. al Coda

CODA

F   C/E G7sus/D C

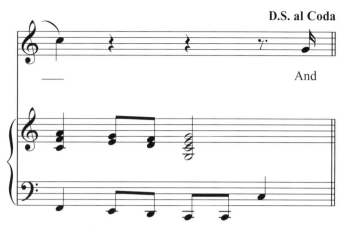

And

Yeah, let it be, ___

Am   Cmaj7/G   F   C

___ let it be, ___   let it be, _____ yeah, let it be. ___   Oh,

G   **1**   F   C/E G7sus/D C

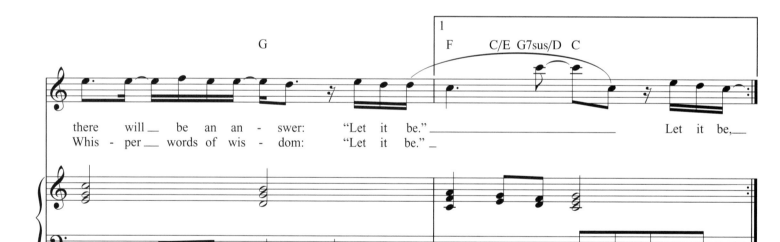

there will __ be an an - swer: "Let it be." _____   Let it be, ___
Whis - per __ words of wis - dom: "Let it be." _

2 F   C/E G7sus/D C   F   C/E G7sus/D C   B♭ F/A   G   F   C

rit.